CHAIN REACTIONS IN CRIMINAL JUSTICE

CHAIN REACTIONS IN CRIMINAL JUSTICE

Discretion and the Necessity of Interdisciplinary Research

A shorter version of this text was presented as a lecture
held on the occasion of accepting
the Ada and Paul Cornil Prize
at the Vrije Universiteit Brussel on March 12, 2015

by

Professor Maartje van der Woude

eleven
international publishing

Published, sold and distributed by Eleven International Publishing
P.O. Box 85576
2508 CG The Hague
The Netherlands
Tel.: +31 70 33 070 33
Fax: +31 70 33 070 30
e-mail: sales@elevenpub.nl
www.elevenpub.com

Sold and distributed in USA and Canada
International Specialized Book Services
920 NE 58th Avenue, Suite 300
Portland, OR 97213-3786, USA
Tel: 1-800-944-6190 (toll-free)
Fax: +1-503-280-8832
orders@isbs.com
www.isbs.com

Eleven International Publishing is an imprint of Boom uitgevers Den Haag.

ISBN 978-94-6236-714-2
ISBN 978-94-6274-625-1 (E-book)

Cover image: Federico Andreotti, *Discretion, The Better Part Of Valour*

Printed in The Netherlands

PREFACE

"And to the degree that the individual puts up a show before others that he himself does not believe in, he can come to experience a special kind of alienation from self and a special kind of wariness of others."
– Erving Goffman: The Presentation of Self in Everyday Life (1959)

Criminologists are all aware of the dangers of labeling. Individuals may be determined or influenced by the terms used to describe or to classify them, which can eventually cause them to start acting upon the dominant label used for their classification. I have always been averse to labels. Often have I been asked the question: "But what are you? Do you consider yourself to be a legal scholar, a socio-legal scholar or a criminologist?" Being something in between, an interdisciplinary scholar, just didn't seem to be an option. Yet for me pretending to be monodisciplinary felt like putting on a show I personally did not believe in. Whereas I used to get somewhat insecure by questions like this, I have grown comfortable with my hybrid nature and, as I will elaborate upon later on, I am of the opinion that to fully grasp the complexity of many criminal justice matters, much research would benefit from closer ties between legal and empirical scholarship (Van der Woude 2012).

Being able to write this booklet, which is a slightly more elaborate version of my lecture held on accepting the Ada and Paul Cornil Prize at the Vrije Universiteit Brussel on March 12, 2015, is further confirmation that refusing to choose in the past has, in fact, been the right choice for me.[1] I am greatly honored to have been awarded the Ada and Paul Cornil Prize, for which I owe Professor Kristel Beyens and Professor Sonja Snacken my deepest gratitude. By stimulating further research in the field of criminological sociology as well as the field of criminal policy, the prize also promotes further integration of legal and social sciences. Therefore while receiving this prize is a great honor, I also feel that meeting the task that accepting it entails is a great responsibility.

By presenting both my past and current research, as well as some broader reflections on where both collide around the concept of discretion, I hope to stimulate some discussion, hopefully leading to closer research ties, not just between the disciplines of criminal law, criminology and sociology, but more importantly, between both our universities and specifically the Crime and Society Research Group (VUB), the Institute for Criminal Law and Criminology and the Van Vollenhoven Institute for Law, Governance and Society (both part of Leiden Law School).

1 The Vrije Universiteit Brussel awards the Ada and Paul Cornil prize once every four years to stimulate scientific research in the field of criminological sociology and criminal policy.

TABLE OF CONTENTS

1. DISCRETION AS AN INTERDISCIPLINARY CONCEPT

Recent years have shown some, not many, products of true interdisciplinary research collaborations between scholars of criminal law and criminologists. Looking at the products of these successful collaborations, they always seem to revolve around one central concept or phenomenon that resonates in both the field of the law and of the social sciences. The concepts of legitimacy and criminalization are probably the most notable examples in that sense, with the former – legitimacy – topping the charts due to a strong interdisciplinary research line on procedural justice (see for instance: Tankebe & Liebling 2013). I would like to introduce another one of those concepts that is perfectly fit to be subjected to an interdisciplinary analysis that combines insights from the realm of the criminal and other law with those from the field of criminology and sociology of laws. One could even argue that it is necessary to subject this concept to this analysis. It is the concept of discretion and discretionary decision-making.

DEFINING DISCRETION IN MATTERS OF CRIMINAL JUSTICE

While ordinary decision-making involves choosing when and how to intervene or act, discretionary decision-making refers to deciding to act or not when the circumstances legally allow for it. Perhaps the most well-known illustration of discretionary decision-making was put forward by Dworkin (1977) when he stated that discretion is similar to a hole in a doughnut: it does not exist save for a belt of restriction surrounding it. It has historically been thought that the law imposes the most important belt of restriction. The truth of this assumption, as I will argue, is debatable. Law or legal restrictions are just one of multiple factors restricting one's discretionary decision. According to Kanstroom (2003), it might be more accurate to refer to discretion as the coffee into which the doughnut is dipped as discretion should be seen as the juncture between legal practice and some sort of extra-legal realm of justice. In an attempt to formulate a clear definition of discretion, Gelsthorpe and Padfield (2004: 3) in their published edited collection Exercising Discretion – which overall has been a great inspiration for my own thinking on this topic – state that "(…) discretion refers to the freedom, power, authority, decision or leeway of an official, organization or individual to decide, discern or determine to make a judgment, choice or decision, about alternative courses of action or inaction." It is not the aim of this lecture to provide an overview of the various definitions of discretion that have been used by scholars over time. Yet it is important to note here that discretion is an exceptionally fluid concept and that it revolves around the core notion of choice. For discretion to exist, an official must be given power, within a broad framework, to either choose the end which is to be pursued or, if the end has already been determined, to choose the most appropriate means or standard to achieve the end. Galligan calls this process of creating standards "individuation" and the – often implicit – standards created, which serve as guides to decision-making, as "principles of individuation" (Galligan 1976). How much discretion an official has will depend on the nature of the power and the extent to which other officials recognize his authority to choose (Mensah 1998).

As a result of fundamental changes in the nature of modern society, the state is called upon to intervene in many areas of social life, and the issues that have to be grappled with are inherently complex (Unger 1976; Prosser 1982; Beck 1992; Giddens 1999). Both the diversity and the complexity of problems that states have to deal with in modern society require a flexible approach. Therefore, in order to meet the demands that are being made on the modern state, discretion, rather than rules, seems to be the better mechanism for exercising power. The institution of state control that applies the most direct form of power is without a doubt the criminal justice system. Criminal justice systems rely heavily on official granting of discretionary power. Considerable discretionary authority is vested in criminal justice bureaucracies to make and to implement policy. Judges, prosecutors, public officials, and lawyers all exercise some form of discretion in their daily decision-making on matters of criminal law and criminal justice cases (Hawkins 1992).

As Hawkins notes: "discretionary power resides at all levels of criminal justice bureaucracies. From the most senior officials at the center who frame broad policy, to the most junior recruits at street level whose work as screening or gatekeeping officials means direct contact with the difficulties of the real world." (Hawkins 1992, p. 12). It is at street level where discretionary power not only permits the realization of the law's broad purposes, but where officials sometimes are allowed or even encouraged to distort the word or spirit of the law or policy, or to ignore them (Hawkins 1992). Street-level bureaucrats, defined here as personnel working for criminal justice agencies who have regular direct contact with members of the public, such as police officers or probation officers, are the final implementers of public policy. Their jobs are inherently discretionary (Prottas

1979; Lipsky 2010; Maynard-Moody & Musheno 2003) and the decisions they make directly affect the distribution of justice. A street-level bureaucrat's justice judgment, i.e. his or her conception of what justice requires in any given situation, may affect other people's lives for better or worse in very significant ways (Maynard-Moody & Portillo 2010).

As I will discuss later on, much of the research on discretion and discretionary decision-making tends to focus on the injustice caused by the abuse or misuse of their discretionary powers by law enforcement officials due to the element of subjective choice inherent in discretion. Concerns that bureaucratic discretion may lead to arbitrariness, inconsistencies, unpredictability, and decisions based on officials' personal predilections have been commonplace ever since the displacement of the Weberian bureaucrat as the model of bureaucratic behavior. Correspondingly, the call has traditionally been to limit and confine that discretion (Black 2001). Whereas the risk of arbitrariness is obviously present, I find it important to stress that it is often too easily forgotten that discretion and discretionary decision-making are not only necessary for an efficient functioning of the criminal justice system, they also contribute to justice itself. Given the widespread recognition of the inevitability and necessity of discretion, it seems rather telling that Davis (1975: 33) – one of the authorities on discretionary law – feels compelled to use emphasis in his empirical claim that "every government has always been a government of laws and men." In other words, whereas law and discretion are sometimes presented and even defined as absolute in-kind opposites (Spader 1984), such an image fails to recognize the fact that both law and discretion are necessary in order for criminal and other justice systems to function properly and to be just.

As many have argued, discretion and legal rules are not in a zero sum relationship whereby the more rules there are, the less discretion there is and vice versa. Discretion is something that can be present in degrees (Spader 1984; Dworkin 1977: 31-39; 68-71; for criticism see Galligan 1986: 14-20). But it is always present to a lesser or greater extent than one might think, and is exercised in places that one might not expect. Far from being easy to confine or structure using rules, rules and discretion operate in a complex interrelationship (Baldwin and Hawkins 1984; Galligan 1986; Hawkins 1992b; Bell 1992; Schneider 1992; Black 1997). Discretion is therefore inherently neither good nor bad. It can be used skillfully to counter ill-conceived or vague laws and policies, or to minimize wrongful arrests and convictions, excessive punishments, and failures to bring culpable offenders to justice. But it can be misused as well, with immediate harm to the victims of the abuse and long-lasting harm to the legitimacy of our system of criminal justice. In his seminal work, *The Collapse of American Criminal Justice*, the late William Stuntz illustrates how both too much and too little discretion have had disastrous effects on the legitimacy of the criminal justice system of the United States (Stuntz 2011). Research on discretion is therefore vital to manage and control discretion. I hope this rather brief and therefore somewhat unpolished outline of discretion and discretionary decision-making at least clarifies why they are such interesting concepts for scholars of criminal law as well as social scientists. Academics from both disciplines need each other to make sense of the complex triangular tension between the legal framework, human interpretation and social context within which the interpretation of the legal framework takes place. Yet so far most of the available research doesn't seem to reflect this complexity much.

Although the concept of discretion is indeed studied in various disciplines, there seems to be little dialogue between scholars working within the various fields (Bell 1992). Whereas there seems to be some cross-fertilization between the various strands of social science research on discretion (Hupe 2013), there seems to be a disconnect between legal scholars studying the concept and "the" social sciences. In his attempt to bridge the gap between the social sciences and the law with regard to studying discretion, Hawkins (1992: 18) observes that those who work in jurisprudence and law are concerned with clarifying conceptual issues or devising methods for the control of discretion while being concerned with "decision-making procedures and the scope for the play of individual judgement afforded within a structure of rules (…) also with the nature of discretionary power, with the ways in which official authority is used, and with questions of legitimacy" (Davis 1969; Dworkin 1977; Galligan 1986; Handler 1986). By approaching discretion in this way, Hawkins (1992: 18) notes that legal scholars seem to approach discretion as if it were not only a property of individual behavior, but also essentially guided by legal rules. They do not usually contemplate the many other forces that influence criminal justice decision-makers. Whereas discretion is obviously heavily implicated in the use of legal rules, the very nature of these rules, their need for interpretation in application, means that legal rules are shot through with discretion. Therefore, how decision-makers come to their decisions is and can only be partly determined by legal rules. Organizational norms and practices, past experiences, personal relationships, the decision-maker's own perceptions and attitudes will all play a part in affecting how decisions are made (Lipsky 1980, 2010). Thus the presence of legal rules does not mean that these rules will be the sole or even dominant factor influencing how discretion is exercised, and their absence does not mean that the decision-maker is not bound by his or her decision: bureaucratic and organizational norms will continue to operate, as will broader political and economic pressures, and personal moral and social norms. (Hawkins, 1992a, 1992b, 1986; Galligan 1986; Black 1997b)

Where legal scholars have shown little concern for the actual behavior of those who exercise criminal justice discretion, social scientists have frequently been guilty of discounting the part played by legal rules in shaping discretion while explaining the outcomes of decision-making processes. Studies in this area seem to take for granted that law is not a discrete social phenomenon, but that its importance lies in its interactions with other social factors. As Padfield, Liebling and Arnold (2004) rightfully observe, identifying where formal – legal – discretion begins and ends is a central task to any research concerned with process and discretionary decision-making. While referring to Barnet (1981), Hawkins (1992: 19) states that "law enforcement official's discretion is more clearly imprinted by the nature and form of the legal rules they work with than at first thought, even if such influence is not necessarily exerted in ways that might be intended by legislatures or legal bureaucracies." Empirical scholars have mostly been concerned with showing how outcomes are produced in handling cases in criminal justice by studying not discretion but the decision-making of legal actors. In doing so, empirical scholars tend to understand the decision-making process by looking at its outcomes and by establishing the "criteria" or "factors" said to have been taken into account in making particular choices. Whereas empirical insight in decision-making is highly valuable in understanding those instances when law enforcement officials seem to decide on the basis of forces other than legal rules, it risks oversimplifying matters. According to several scholars (Hupe 2013; Meyers & Nielsen 2012; Jewel & Glaser 2006; Hawkins 2002, 2003), discretionary decisions can only be understood when placed in the context of (1) the broad social and political situation in which decision-making activities take place; (2) the legal and organizational setting within the surroundings that serves as the defined setting in which decisions are made; and (3) an official's individual decision frame, shaped by a variety of personal features such as a persons moral blueprint and beliefs. Therefore, in order to fully understand and to justly analyze discretionary decision-making, it is necessary that legal and empirical scholars join forces.

A CHAIN OF DISCRETION THROUGHOUT THE CRIMINAL JUSTICE SYSTEM

In line with the necessity to take a broader – multi-factor – approach when studying discretion or discretionary decision-making and focusing on the interaction of the various factors, studies also need to move beyond the single actor and single-case level and towards systemic comparisons across different settings and contexts (Hupe 2013; Meyers & Nielsen 2012; Jewel & Glaser 2006). In legal and empirical studies, discretion or discretionary decision-making is often also studied in isolation by focusing on the actions of one particular criminal justice actor, most often police officials, prosecutors or judges. As Hawkins argues (1992, 2003), discretionary decision-making in criminal justice matters should be seen as a collective enterprise and so it is important to move towards a more systemic or holistic view of discretion by looking at the way in which cases move throughout a decision-making system, and at interaction between cases or groups of cases. Discretion is part of a sequence of decisions and it takes place as part of a network of relationships in the legal system (Emerson 1983; Emerson & Paley 1992). What may on the surface appear to be one simple discretionary decision quite often involves a rather more complex series of decisions. It is important to recognize the existence of interaction between the various actors within the system, that the "output" for one actor provides the "input" for another (Hupe 2013; Meyers & Nielsen 2012; Jewel & Glaser 2006; Hawkins 1992, 2003). Reitz (1998) speaks of "the hydraulic displacement of discretion between actors." A more systemic, or serial, approach towards discretion also draws attention to the fact that effective powers to decide are frequently assumed by actors other than the person allocated formal authority to exercise discretion. Discretion is diffused among a variety of actors that all play a part in the handling of an individual case. As a result of this diffusion, it becomes difficult to conceive the visible official point of decision being the place at which real discretion was exercised. The diffusion of discretion means that the power to make discretionary decisions is dispersed among a series of actors involved in criminal justice decision-making. With this in mind, a set of actors that tends to be overlooked as important in the chain of discretionary decision-making are the legislature and criminal justice policymakers. As I mentioned earlier, discretionary decisions are not only made by law enforcement officials such as police officers, prosecutors or judges, but also by criminal justice policymakers and legislative officials. According to Galligan (1986: 18), "the very heart of the discretionary process lies within legislative and policy decisions." In line with Galligan, Schneider (1992) is of the opinion that discretion should be viewed as being deliberately built in to decision-making systems. Whereas legislative decisions shape the formal legal framework of discretion, it is subsequently shaped and transferred down throughout an organizational hierarchy through policy. Policy, like legal rules, acts therefore as one of the constraints in the context or field within which individual decisions have to be made. In an attempt to identify productive new directions for criminological research that can link the discretion of key criminal justice actors to important criminal justice outcomes like crime levels, justice and racial disparity, Bushway and Forst (2013) introduce a new conceptualization of discretion that aims to respect both its interdisciplinary nature as well as its systemic nature. They distinguish between what they refer to as "Type A" and "Type B" discretion with Type A discretion referring to the discretion that individual actors have to make decisions with variation given a set of rules, and Type B to the discretion that legislators and criminal justice policymakers have to establish a set of rules. The decision by legislators to impose sentencing guidelines is an act of Type B discretion; when judges select a sentence from the legally allowable sentences within the sentencing guideline, they are exercising Type A discretion. Type B discretion, the ability to create rules and policies, can be used to limit and shape Type A discretion, and there is often tension between the rules set by higher-level, administrative actors (Type B) and the discretion within those rules that is available to lower level actors, including those at street level, who are responsible for the actual enforcement of the rules. Most discussion in the literature deals with Type A discretion, yet according to Bushway and Forst (2013), it is Type B discretion that deserves more direct study in criminal justice. They illustrate their claim by pointing out the powerful influence that state legislators have in the USA:

"The states in the USA clearly have a great deal of Type B discretion to set sentencing rules that fall within the general guidelines of constitutionality, and the exercise of this discretion by legislators has led to a huge variation across states in the basic structure of sentencing. This variation is potentially more influential than variation in Type A discretion of individual actors within any given set of rules." (Bushway & Forst 2013: 201)

By focusing on various "layers" in the decision-making process and the interaction between those layers, Bushway and Forst's definition of discretion also underlines the importance of a closer connection, or at least a closer communication between, legal and empirical scholars researching discretion and discretionary decision-making.

In the following I will use the distinction between Types A and B discretion as a somewhat artificial analytical "tool" to structure my argument. In reality, as I will also conclude, these two strands, or levels, of discretionary decision-making interact, not only with each other, but also with a broader legal, organizational and social context. By drawing from my research on Dutch counterterrorism legislation (Van der Woude 2010) I will first elaborate on Type B discretion and the potentially unnecessarily negative conclusions resulting from studying criminal justice decision-making only at the legislative and policy level. Subsequently, I will reflect on the broad strand of research aimed at analyzing ethno-racial profiling. This research is mostly concerned with Type A discretion and – as I will argue – therefore tends to entail the risk of perhaps too readily drawing firm and potentially damaging conclusions about the integrity and legitimacy of the actions of law enforcement officials. I will discuss my latest research on the merging of crime control and immigration control, a process also known as "crimmigration" (Stumpf 2006; Van der Leun 2010; Van der Woude, Van der Leun & Nijland 2014) in the third part of this booklet. This interdisciplinary phenomenon cannot be fully understood without paying attention to both Type A and Type B discretion and the way in which the two interact with each other. Since the modest aim of this booklet is to present a potential direction for future interdisciplinary research in the field of criminal law and criminology by presenting a variety of research projects that all focus on the concept of discretion, it seems somewhat odd to close with a conclusion. The conclusion has already been presented in this introduction: there is a need for more cross-fertilization between the legal and the empirical disciplines in order to make sense of one of the most central concepts to criminal justice systems worldwide. Instead, I will close with some reflections on how to encourage and effectuate further interdisciplinary research on discretion.

2. UNFORESEEN OPENINGS IN THE IRON CAGE OF ACTUARIAL JUSTICE AND "EXCEPTIONAL" CONTROL

In the period from 2005 to 2010, I studied the decisions made by the Dutch legislature in response to the "new" terrorism as the world has come to know since the attacks in the United States on September 11th 2001 (Van der Woude 2010). Looking only at the realm of Dutch criminal law, in a relatively short period of time – give or take 5 years – an impressive body of counter-terrorism legislation has been drafted and implemented by the Dutch legislature. The Netherlands was already faced with terrorism in the form of the so-called "South Moluccan actions" in the 1970s. Through a series of violent incidents against Dutch and Indonesian targets, the Free South Molucca Youth aimed to restore South Moluccan independence from Indonesia by establishing an independent Republic of the South Moluccas, the RMS (Republik Maluku Selatan) (Bootsma 2000; Janse 2005).

Since the legislature back then decided that, despite the social unrest and casualties resulting from this political violence, it wasn't necessary to respond with new legislation or by expanding existing laws and powers, I was interested in uncovering the reasons why. On the contrary, the government back then responded with a policy based on dialogue and negotiation, also known as "the Dutch approach". Under this approach, resorting to far-reaching repression on the part of the national police or the military was considered to be a last resort. As a result the government at the time did not feel it was necessary to assign more or more extensive powers to law enforcement authorities (Borgers & Van Sliedregt 2009; Van der Woude 2010). A major difference between fighting terrorism in the 1970s and nowadays is that, since September 11 2001, the government has pinned its faith on the creating broad criminal liability by criminalizing the preliminary stages before a terrorist act takes place, focusing on the purpose for which a certain action is performed. Post 9/11 measures have also resulted in a broadening of investigative powers by lowering the threshold that has to be met by law enforcement officials before they can start an overt or covert criminal investigation. The "Dutch approach" to negotiation has faded completely into the background (Van der Woude 2010; Borgers & Van Sliedregt 2009). Obviously, post 9/11 terrorism differs from the Moluccan terrorism in the sense that the latter was not religiously inspired and that it remained confined to the Netherlands as a movement. In terms of casualties, the Moluccan actions may even be considered more dangerous: the two train hijackings and the occupation of a primary school claimed more victims in the Netherlands than the Islamic terrorism that has held the world in its grip since the attacks on the Pentagon and the World Trade Center.

The pursuit of security and (subjective) safety has become the major objective as well as the justification for many new policies and legislation (Simon 2007). This field of criminal law, in particular, has been "awarded" an important role in this political pursuit, and has consequently contributed to the development of what has come to be known as actuarial criminal justice. Actuarial criminal justice refers to the development of preventive criminal justice. Actuarial criminal law takes insecurity as the underlying value of security politics, operating on the basis of permanent feelings of fear, anxiety and unease. Security discourses and policies in the culture of control are increasingly dominated by the logic of risk management, a logic which calls for the management and government of risky populations using statistical calculations and proactive management rather than through the reactive management of real events and threats (Van Munster 2004). Actuarial criminal justice links coercive state actions to suspicion without the need for a charge, prosecution or conviction. It also includes measures that expand the remit of criminal law to include activities or associations that are deemed to precede the actual substantive offence targeted for prevention. Clearly, the starting point of actuarial justice is prevention rather than defense against the actual threat. This means that the use and desirability of preventive action is placed in the foreground, also where it concerns criminal law. As Dutch legal scholars Borgers and Van Sliedregt (2010: 172-173) justly note, this development is "foreign" to the criminal law system in a certain sense.

It is safe to say that all Dutch counterterrorism laws were severely criticized both by external critics – mostly legal scholars – as well as by some politicians in the preliminary stages of the legislative procedure. Whereas the first group was quite consistent in voicing its concerns about the legitimacy, the necessity and the potential undesirable and dangerous side effects of these new laws, initially critical politicians seemed less likely to stick to their guns. After being reassured by the Minister of Security and Justice's standard motivation that "the proposed measures and powers are necessary in view of the threat that international terrorism poses for democratic Dutch society," they would magically waive their concerns to vote positively on behalf of the proposed bill in question (Van der Woude 2010, 2012). It was in the work of Garland, *The Culture of Control* (2001), the work of Simon and Feeley on the rise of a new penology and the development of actuarial justice (1992; 1994), and the work of Giorgio Agamben on the emergence and consequences of a perpetual state of emergency around crime and security (1998, 2001) that I found valuable insights that may explain the legislature's remarkable decisions post 9/11.

ACTUARIALISM, EXCEPTIONALISM AND CONTROL INFLUENCING LEGISLATIVE CHOICES[2]

Besides offering valuable insights, the abovementioned macro level – more abstract – analyses of contemporary penality also paint a rather depressing picture. According to Feeley and Simon, certain pivotal transformations have taken place in penal discourses, objectives and techniques, giving rise to what they termed a "new penology." Feeley and Simon (1992, 1994, 2003) presented the new penology as an analytical grid seeking to give meaning to the transformations that have emerged in the field of American penality over the last 25 years. Increasingly, researchers are wondering about the suitability of the analytical model in the analysis of penality in other areas, such as Canada and Europe (or certain countries in Europe).

As Cheliotis (2006) rightfully observes in line with various other commentators, Feeley and Simon suggest that recent years have seen the demise of the optimistic post-war penal vision of the criminological truth it claimed. Whether referred to as rehabili-

2 This paragraph draws from a previously published book chapter: Woude, M.A.H. van der (2012a) 'Dutch Counterterrorism: An Exceptional Body of Legislation or Just an Inevitable Product of the Culture of Control?' In: G. Molier & A. Ellian (eds.), *The State of Exception in a Time of Terror.* Dordrecht: Republic of Letters Publishing, 69-95.

tative (Allen 1981), penal-welfarist (Garland 1985) or otherwise, the idea of normalizing offenders by instilling moral values and effecting behavioral change, while at the same time facilitating their gradual resettlement into the community "seems utopian and little is done in practice to implement it" (Morris 2002: 195-197). Crime is relieved of its moral connotations, in a view close to the Durkheimian vision of criminality, where crime is an inevitable and accepted phenomenon. Delinquency is seen as a normal risk, of the same type as other risks covered by social security, such as illness or unemployment (Feeley & Simon 1994: 173).

Crime is considered to be a technical problem rather than an individual or social one, the effects of which are more important than the causes. Crime is conceived of as a statistical probability rather than a transgression. The penal process's aim is not to respond to individual deviance or to social problems, but to regulate the levels of deviance, to minimize the occurrence and negative consequences of crimes, and thus to render crime tolerable through systemic management (Feeley & Simon 1992: 452 and 455; Slingeneyer 2010; Robert 2001: 77; Lynch 1998: 842). Responding to the need for increased accountability and rationality, the new penal totem is that security, or at least a gloss of it, can be reinforced through the effective regulation of designated risk groups and efficient system management. In multiple ways and on multiple stages, the system deploys actuarial techniques that assess offenders not as coherent subjects, but as members of particularly risky or dangerous subpopulations. As a result of this actuarial logic, the penal system has moved from a language based on the morality of the offender to a language based on probability and statistical distribution within the population (Feeley & Simon 1992: 452). With rehabilitative ideals thrown out of the window, under the new penology criminal justice, decision-making seems to be increasingly dehumanized and reduced to risk calculations and assessments based on broad categorizations and group stereotypes.

In line with Feeley and Simon, *The Culture of Control* (Garland 2001) paints an equally grim picture. According to Rumgay (2003: 44) Garland presents a "depressive analysis" in which "all things seem to conspire to the same regrettable ends." Garland's analysis is intended as an explanation for a radical change in the approach to crime and ideas about it.[3] In order to fully grasp the impact of the culture of control, it is important to understand that the new field of crime control and criminal justice was shaped not by the programs of reformers or by criminological ideas, but by the character of late twentieth-century society, its problems, its culture and its technologies of power (Garland 2001: 72). According to Garland, the social, economic and cultural changes associated with late modernity are the root cause for the changes within the field of crime control and criminal justice policy that have become visible since the mid-seventies. Whereas these changes have had a profound positive effect on the welfare state and its institutions, they have also had a negative side effect in the form of crime. The relaxation of informal social and situational controls in all areas of life, the general

3 Garland observes twelve indices of changes within crime control since the seventies that typify the culture of control: the decline of the rehabilitative ideal; the re-emergence of punitive sanctions and expressive justice; changes in the emotional tone of crime policy; the return of the victim – above all: the public must be protected; politicization and the new populism; the reinvention of the prison; the transformation of criminological thought; the expanding infrastructure of crime prevention and community safety; civil society and the commercialization of crime control; new management styles and working practices; and a perceptual sense of crisis (Garland 2001: 6-20).

increase in material wealth and the presence of a large "population at risk" – teenage males with great affluence and mobility outside the disciplines of work and family and used to instant gratification – have led to more opportunities to commit crimes and to a more crime-prone society in general (Garland 2000; also Bauman 2000). Crime has become yet another product of late-modern society, a part of everyday experienced reality. A multiplicity of developments have contributed to the fact that the focus of criminal justice and law is no longer the rehabilitation of individuals demonstrating deviant behavior, but rather the protection of the majority in society that do behave in line with the law. Most attention is now paid to controlling crime and the risks of crime. The use of criminal law as an instrument to control safety risks has become part of an all-encompassing culture of control. According to Garland, the notion that crime in late modern societies has become a normal fact of life has led to the formation of a distinctive culture that has developed around crime – a culture that changes the conditions in which criminal law and criminal justice policy operate.

This cultural formation, which is referred to as the crime control complex of late modernity, is characterized by a distinctive cluster of attitudes, beliefs and practices. Citizens become crime conscious, attuned to the crime problem, and exhibit high levels of fear and anxiety. Fear of crime is sufficiently widespread to become a political reference point, and crime issues are generally politicized and represented in emotive terms (Garland 2001: 163). A high level of "crime consciousness" has come to be embedded in everyday social life and institutionalized in the media, in popular culture and the architecture of urban areas (see also: Altheide 2003). Garland describes how citizens' engagement with crime and crime control is somewhat ambivalent. Whereas people seem to partially adapt to the situation of increased crime being the "new normal" by developing new habits of avoidance and crime prevention routines, the new normal also creates frustration and aggravation because of the cumulative nuisance it represents for daily life. The trauma of powerlessness in the face of fear prompts the demand for action. The feeling that "something must be done" and "someone must be blamed" increasingly finds representation and fuels political action, resulting in symbolic and expressive actuarial criminal justice policies aimed at allaying public fear and concerns by giving the impression that risky situations and individuals should and can be identified in order to warrant security (Van der Woude 2012). This is where the probabilistic logic of the new penology meets, and neatly fits in with, the logic of the culture of control.

The State of Exception (Agamben 2004) investigates the increase of power structures that governments employ in supposed times of crisis. Within these times of crisis, Agamben refers to increased extension of power as states of exception, where questions of citizenship, civil liberties and individual rights can be diminished, superseded and rejected in the process of claiming this extension of power by a government. The state of exception invests one person or a government with the power and voice of authority over others, and it is extended well beyond where the law existed in the past. The development of actuarial justice as a common feature of the culture of control fits this description. Motivated by the pursuit of absolute safety, governments go to great lengths to detect criminal and risky behavior in the earliest stage possible, even if this entails an infringement of certain civil liberties. Actuarial criminal justice is one of the means through which governments expand their grip on all possible human behavior, including potentially risky or criminal behavior. This expansion of the government's net of social control through actuarial justice in a culture of control is also accompanied by a dispersal of discipline because crime control has been extended to local and non-governmental agencies (Cohen 1979, 1985). Due to this extended capacity for influence and action, governments in a culture of control clearly become more powerful than before: they are able to fully control all citizens and to decide who should be excluded from society or at least deprived of their civil liberties and rights because they are a potential risk or threat (Hudson 2003). Or, to speak in Agamben's terms, to actively separate "political beings" (citizens) from "bare life" (bodies).

Taken together *State of Exception* and *Culture of Control* shine a light on various important legal transformations. The state of exception is no longer a strictly legal category, as it is in the constitutional sense of a "state of siege," yet it coincides with the emergence of a culture of control. The merging of the culture of control and the state of exception has profound consequences for the drafting of new legislation and policies within the field of criminal justice. Whereas Garland's thesis has shown that politicians and policymakers have to and do respond to the new criminological predicament of late modern societies through various types of policies and laws, by focusing mainly on the outcome he does not explicitly address the way in which this new predicament has also affected the policymaking process itself. This dynamic is made clearer in Agamben's work. One of the basic problems of the state of exception is in fact the continued intrusion of the executive power in the legislature (Agamben 2003: 18). Agamben even argues that politics has "contaminated itself with law" in the state of exception.[4] The political power over others acquired through the state of exception places the government as allpowerful, operating outside of the laws. During such times of extension of power, certain forms of knowledge are respected and accepted as true, and certain voices are considered valuable, while many others are not. These political dynamics could negatively affect the legislature and the legislative procedure in such a way that the outcome of the legislative procedure in a culture of control with regard to new criminal legislation becomes a foregone conclusion. Instead of being the result of a process of carefully weighing and balancing various competing interests and values, new criminal legislation and crime policies are motivated solely by irrational fears, "gut feelings" and incident-oriented political impetus in order to win elections.

As a result of its emphasis on risk control and prevention, the culture of control institutionalizes the state of exception as a permanent aspect of global order. Following Van Munster, in it,

> "Sovereignty is constituted in a Schmittian sense as much as bare life is subjected to actuarial criminal justice which goes hand in hand with technological processes of risk identification, administration and assessment. The dispersal and expansion of surveillance society implies that heterogeneous factors and events such as place of birth, religion, travel records, reading records, visa applications and immigration all become part of a cybernetics of control in which risk information is intrinsic to all decisions made on these issues. Prevention then is not concerned with the production of something good. Its aim is to repress anxiety and fear.

4 www.youtube.com/watch?v=ks-us_H2gGI (last visited July 27 2016).

It does not work towards some utopian goal, but is guided by the principle of apocalypse." (Van Munster 2004: 152-153)

The culture of control is a catastrophic society. In it the exceptional condition has become the norm. It cannot be denied that this conclusion is rather depressing. Reflecting on Garland's thesis, the root cause for the current culture of control can be found in the great structural and cultural changes brought about by late modernity. Since these changes cannot be reversed and time will have to tell whether future cultural and structural changes will change the current social dynamics, it seems as if we are simply stuck in an exceptional culture of control ruled by subjective fears of dangerous others whom we hope to identify before they succumb to their criminal urges. Now that the legislature – the institutional foundation of the criminal justice apparatus, the backbone of all further decisions on criminal justice – has become so "contaminated" by the dynamics of the crime complex, producing predominantly actuarial laws and policies that, due to their pre-emptive nature are also often characterized by a great amount of discretion given to "street-level" police officers and other law enforcement agents, the late modern criminal justice apparatus seems to be set up for failure in the form of due process and human rights violations. This is especially so when it comes to dealing with a high-profile "global risk" such as terrorism (Beck 2002). While referring to the movie Minority Report, McCulloch and Pickering (2009) state that counterterrorism advances a pre-crime logic aimed at pre-empting latent threats, a form of "justice through the crystal ball', with all its worrying consequences.

PERHAPS NOT SO STUCK IN AN IRON CAGE: THE ROLE OF HUMAN AGENCY IN A CULTURE OF CONTROL

As noted, many academics were very concerned about the way in which Dutch counterterrorism legislation and policies would play out in practice, especially the expanded investigatory and discretionary powers given to the police and intelligence services resulting from the newly implemented laws. Fears for unjust – ethno-racial – profiling and other forms of wrongful use of power were repeatedly expressed. In 2009, a committee of independent experts pointed out the necessity for an integral and interdisciplinary evaluation of all measures. They were not only concerned about the necessity and the legitimacy of the measures, but also explicitly mentioned their potentially negative side effects, such as polarization and stigmatization (Suyver Committee 2009). Despite the committee's explicit recommendation to empirically assess these side effects, for they might even further contribute to the process of radicalization and thus leading to more terrorism, the Ministry for Security and Justice largely refused to follow the committee's recommendations. The legislation was evaluated by the Ministry itself instead of by an external, hence more objective, party and only addressed matters of legitimacy. The concerns about negative side effects were not addressed at all. So far, the developments around Dutch counterterrorism still seem to confirm the iron cage dynamics. Responding to and feeding the public fear of terrorism, very few politicians seemed to be willing to take a critical stance. In the wake of the rise of so-called Islamic State and the string of attacks occurring in Europe, it seems unlikely that this will change anytime soon. Yet, although the debates on terrorism and counterterrorism are highly publicized, politicized and emotional, and the measures taken are strongly actuarial, preventive and discretionary, this doesn't mean that we're left to the whims of electorally driven politicians and fearful citizens. Looking past the level of political decision-making, looking past the legislative level to the enforcement level showed some unforeseen openings in the Dutch iron cage of counterterrorism.

In 2014, an evaluation of the most controversial counterterrorism Act was published – Act on the Extension of the Scope for Investigation and Prosecution of Terrorist Crimes (WODC 2014). This Act firmly expanded the investigative powers that can be used if there are "indications" of terrorism. "Indications" can be based on anonymous tips, rumors that are hard to verify, intelligence, etc. Reasonable suspicion is not required, as a result of which the threshold to use these intrusive powers is not only very low, but also very discretionary. Surprisingly enough, with regard to the actual use of the newly introduced investigative powers, the evaluation showed that these powers had only been used to a very limited extent, and some had not been used so far by those agencies tasked with the Act's enforcement. When asked for an explanation, respondents stated that it had not been necessary to use the new powers since existing powers were sufficient, or that they didn't feel comfortable using the new powers because of the lack of case-law and, with this, the lack of clarity on their scope. Instead of over-using, misusing or abusing these new and often highly discretionary powers, law enforcement officials seemed to avoid using them because of their discretionary nature. Police officials aren't the only ones resisting the iron cage by deciding not use certain powers that most politicians believe are highly necessary in the light of the current terrorism. One of the strongest critical voices against Dutch counterterrorism legislation came from the judiciary. On various occasions and in different institutional structures, members of the judiciary have expressed their concerns about the development of a highly discretionary criminal justice apparatus leading to "Gesinnungsstrafrecht" – criminalizing thoughts instead of actions – and dragnet investigations guided by religious and ethnic stereotypes, as a result of which certain groups in society would have to prove their innocence before being found guilty. With politicians largely ignoring their concerns, the Dutch courts are rather reluctant, or better said extremely careful, when interpreting Dutch counterterrorism legislation. In the still limited, albeit steadily growing, number of terrorism cases, there are many examples of the court explicitly addressing the need to restrictively interpret the various criminal provisions. By using their judicial discretion, the courts are also actively resisting the oppressive iron cage (Van der Woude 2012b). Although the weight of the iron cage might soon become too heavy to resist in the light of recent so called Islamic State or Islamic State "inspired" atrocities happening in Europe and the rest of the world, it is important to acknowledge the active role that criminal justice actors can play, and indeed do play, in the broader development of the criminal justice system and the workings of the criminal justice apparatus.

PRELIMINARY CONCLUSION I

The unmistakable power of human agency within criminal justice systems remains unseen and unaccounted for if one only focuses on the macro level, the level of Type B discretionary decision-making. In *Discipline and Punish*, Foucault argues that, "power is not a kind of empty structure stripped of any agents, interests, or grounding nor can it be reduced to bare technological scaffolding" (Foucault 1990: 170-171). In other words, in explaining the formation of certain penal strategies or while analyzing criminal justice processes in general, the role of individuals and agencies in these processes should never be ignored, unlike many macro-level analyses tend to suggest. Researchers need to look at the dialectics of control and resistance within criminal justice organizations themselves.

The characteristics of many Western criminal justice systems nowadays – instrumentalism, actuarialism, populism, control and so forth, all driven by structural and cultural changes feeding populist sentiments in the ongoing "crusade for security" – should not lead us to infer that power structures in contemporary penal organizations are as monolithic and ineluctable as the mechanistic character of managerialism suggests. As Brownlee states, "such a deterministic approach ignores the reflexive agency of the human actor and the capacity for well-placed and charismatic individuals to influence the policy debate, notwithstanding the structural and cultural constraints of action" (1998: 325). Human agency – in other words – can manifest itself as resistance, especially where it concerns the ways in which criminal justice professionals oppose subordination to what may be seen as mechanistic logics and practices of governmental power (Cheliotis 2010: 321).

It is here that the limitations of Ronald Dworkin's often-cited description of discretion – being the hole in the doughnut, non-existing except as an area left open by a surrounding belt of restriction – becomes clear: however elaborate, rules and guidelines cannot exhaustively capture and describe the complexities of all possible contingencies. In all instances of discretionary power, the interpretation and application of supposedly "impersonal" rules are matters to be decided by active, street-level agents who bolster a shared sense of what rules mean by continually working to secure agreement in their practice and "authoritatively enact any of the innumerable possibilities that can plausibly be made out as consistent with rules and precedents" (Barnes 1995: 205). With Cheliotis (2010) I see the exercise of power as a fundamentally associative process involving perpetual negotiation between those placed in positions of dominance and those subordinated in stead of a one-way top-down street. Criminal justice actors at the lower (street) level are dynamic agents who do not merely submit to a power structure. On the contrary, they actively participate in the shaping of that structure through their personal interpretations of legal norms and subsequent decisions. Therefore, being aware of and taking into account the power of human agents to resist and reverse unfortunate turns, wherever and whenever this power is found, is important. Insofar as research aspires to influence the criminal justice policy debate to any significant extent, analyses that fail to identify "the real human stuff of disposition, choice and action, the stuff of which society and history are actually made" (Garland, 2001b: 25), will not – and cannot – be anything other than fatalistic. In doing so, these analyses will even contribute to producing the very crises they are supposed to pre-empt or combat (Cheliotis 2010: 331).

3. ETHNIC PROFILING AS A MEANS TO INTENTIONALLY UNDERMINE JUSTICE?

The previous section has shown that studying only Type B discretionary decision-making by legislatures and policymakers has its limitations if one aims to fully fathom the dynamics of the criminal justice system. In this section, I will address the limitations of only focusing on Type A discretion: the decisions made by street-level bureaucrats working in the field of criminal justice. As noted in the introductory chapter, discretion-wise, the street-level is very interesting for researchers since it is here where the tensions, dilemmas and sometimes contradictions embodied in law and policy are worked out in practice (Hawkins 1992). It is therefore no surprise that there are many studies focusing on the discretionary actions of police officers as the crucial – and most visible – gatekeepers of the criminal justice system. Such a focus can also be justified by insights offered by the theoretical framework of procedural justice (Tyler 2003). Procedural justice is widely considered to be a central factor underlying criminal justice legitimacy. A convincing body of research shows that when police decision-making is perceived as fair, just and respectful, people will be more willing to comply with their instructions, and such perceptions are also directly related to the extent to which people believe that the criminal justice apparatus is legitimate. When people feel that the police are only stopping and checking them because of the color of their skin or ethnic background, this can severely damage their trust in the authorities and their relationship with the police (Tyler & Blader 2003; Tyler & Wakslak 2004; Hough et al. 2010; Hough 2013; Mazerolle et al. 2014). As a result, ethno-racial profiling can also have a negative impact on the effectiveness of policing because citizens don't feel comfortable reporting to or sharing information with the police. Impairing that sort of community intelligence can have grave consequences. For instance, in the Netherlands citizens report about 70 percent of all crime (Van der Veer et al. 2013: 24).

A practice that is considered highly damaging from a procedural justice perspective, and therewith fundamentally damaging for the legitimacy of the criminal justice system, is ethnic or racial profiling by law enforcement officials. "Racial profiling" refers to the use of race as a key factor in police decisions to stop and interrogate citizens without there being objectively justifiable grounds to do so. Most discussions on racial profiling focus on police-initiated stops, although it can also occur in other contexts. The deaths of several African American men and women as a result of police shootings or police brutality in various parts of the United States has recently fuelled debates on the matter, attracting considerable attention from the international mass media, civil rights groups, and political leaders. Eric Garner, Renisha McBride, Amadou Diallo, Rodney King, Michael Brown, Alton Sterling, and Philando Castile are seen as symbols of racially motivated police brutality against the black population in the United States (De Giorgi 2014; Simon 2014). These tragic events and the international media attention they rightfully attracted, in combination with the origins and focus of the bulk of the available research, may suggest that racial profiling is mostly an American problem. Yet tensions between police and minority groups also exist in Europe. The London riots (Solomos 2011), the riots in the banlieus of Parijs (Schneider 2008) as well as the ongoing tensions in multicultural neighborhoods in the city of The Hague in the Netherlands

(Eijkman 2010; Van der Leun et al., 2014) are just a few examples illustrating this. As a result, racial profiling – or ethnic or ethno-racial profiling – is increasingly being publicly debated and researched in Europe as well.

ETHNIC PROFILING IN THE NETHERLANDS?[5]

There are a limited number of studies on proactive policing in the Netherlands that indirectly or directly address ethnic profiling and unequal treatment based on race or nationality (Svensson, Sollie & Saharso 2012; Svensson & Saharso 2014; Çankaya 2012; Kleijer-Kool 2013; Bovenkerk 2014; Van der Leun et al. 2014; Mutsaers 2015; Van der Woude, Brouwer & Dekkers 2016). Proactive police powers are powers to stop and search without requiring reasonable suspicion, making these powers highly discretionary. The goal is to deter criminal activity by showing police presence and engaging the public to learn about their concerns, thereby preventing crime from occurring in the first place. In contrast, responding to a complaint after a crime has been committed is reactive policing. It is safe to say that the notion of proactive policing follows the preventive logic of actuarial justice. Existing Dutch studies consistently show that race and nationality can and often do play a role in proactive police decision-making, yet they also show that there are other factors influencing the decision-making process, such as behav-

5 This paragraph is based on two articles published in Dutch:
1. Dekkers, T.J.M., Leun, J.P. van der & Woude, M.A.H. van der (2015) '"Driving while Black". Lessen en inzichten uit Amerikaans onderzoek naar racial profiling'. *Cahiers Politiestudies* 35 (1): 109-128.
2. Leun, J.P. van der, Woude, M.A.H. van der & Vrijhoed, R. (2015) 'Kleur bekennen, kleur herkennen? Politieopvattingen over de rol van etniciteit bij hun alledaagse beslissingen op straat in drie Haagse wijken'. *Panopticon* 36 (4): 336-352.

ior, clothing, type of vehicle, age, and gender. The importance of a combination of different factors while taking decisions, be they proactive or active, resonates with the findings of international studies on profiling and police decision-making (Johnson & Morgan 2013; Dekkers & Van der Woude 2014). Yet despite the lack of "hard data", a significant part of the Dutch population feels that they are too often being unjustly "hassled" by the police (Coenders et al. 2009; EU FRA 2009). Late 2013, Amnesty International launched two reports stating that ethnic profiling was a pressing matter that the government should deal with immediately (Amnesty International 2013, 2013a). The reports sparked ongoing public and political debates, as a result of which pre-existing taboo on discussing ethnicity in relation to policing in the Netherlands seems to have been broken for good.

MEASURING POLICE DECISION-MAKING THROUGH PERCEPTIONS AND OUTCOMES

PERCEPTIONS

As noted, the debates in the Netherlands were sparked by NGO-initiated reports that were based on the way citizens perceived police actions and police decision-making. This has been an established way to measure ethnic profiling. Led by the Thomas theorem ("If men define situations as real, they are real in their consequences"), by surveying respondents on their personal experiences with ethnic profiling as well as their awareness of people close to them having experienced it, researchers have aimed to get a clearer grasp of the actual scale of this problematic police practice. Based on self-report studies among citizens in the US and other countries, there is considerable evidence that respondents belonging to a minority group believe that law enforcement officers stop them (European Union Agency for Fundamental Rights 2010; Wortley & Owusu-Bempah 2011) or question them (Fitzgerald & Carrington, 2011) more often than they do citizens belonging to the "dominant" (often white) group. Various studies show that these respondents often think that the police stopped or treated them unjustly because of their ethnic background (Jones-Brown 2000; Weitzer & Tuch, 2005; Sollund 2006; Reitzel & Piquero 2006; Parmar 2011; Wortley & Owusu-Bempah 2011). The extent to which certain groups think more negatively about the police might differ per group and per context. Nevertheless, the finding that respondents belonging to minority groups experience more problems with the police than respondents belonging to majority groups is strongly supported in international research (Rice, Reitzel & Piquero 2005). Although the previously mentioned procedural justice framework underlines the necessity to take people's perceptions of reality seriously, one has to be careful about drawing strong conclusions about the actual decision-making process of law enforcement officials based solely on this type of research. This is something researchers should beware of, and something that tends to be disregarded in political and public debates. Some methodological side notes need to be made regarding "perception" research as a way to measure or analyze ethno-racial profiling by street-level law enforcement officers. First, the studies often involve research as a result of which there is generally little understanding of context, meaning and the general inequality of society (Glover 2009). Secondly, whereas the studies do focus on citizens' perceptions, they tend to neglect – or pay significantly less attention to – contemplations and perspectives of other important stakeholders: the law enforcement officials (see Sollund 2005). Thirdly, the perception of being ethno-racially profiled by the police doesn't prove that this is indeed actually happening and, if so, how often. Kennedy (1997) rightfully addresses the importance of distinguishing between "officers who use race as a guide in decision-making and those officers who use race as a discriminatory tool." In order to establish this important distinction – differentiating legitimate from illegitimate policing – it remains to be seen whether the existing research that aims to measure ethnic profiling through the lens of perceptions does justice to the complex context within which street-level law enforcement officers often need to make split-second decisions on a case-by-case basis.

OUTCOMES OF STOPS

Besides perception surveys, there are also numerous studies that focus on the act of profiling itself by examining the outcomes of police stops. These studies are often quantitative. By analyzing what ethnicities are mostly stopped, these studies aim to prove racial profiling is standard practice for the police. As Withrow noticed (2010: 37), "In the history of American policing, no issue has caused more data collection than the issue of racial profiling." Although there is a growing lobby to change this in the Netherlands, unlike in the UK and the US, Dutch police officers do not document the ethnicity of the persons they stop or arrest. In the US and the UK, police officers are required to fill out so-called stop forms on which they have to specify the reason for the stop, the outcome of the stop, the name and the precinct of the officer(s) involved, and the gender, age and ethnicity of the person who was stopped. By systematically keeping track of the ethno-racial background of every person being stopped, this data has served as a vital source of information for large-scale quantitative research projects focusing on racial profiling and aiming to measure it. Yet research has shown that the extent to which police officers are accurate in estimating someone's racial identity tends to vary greatly, which makes it necessary to interpret the results of studies based on this data with great caution. Yet, despite the vast amount of large-scale quantitative research, in their recent synthesis of racial profiling research, Engel and Cohen (2014) reach the conclusion that the empirical answer to the question of whether, and if so to what extent, racial profiling is actually taking place has not been found so far. In line with other authors, they note the methodological challenges in measuring racial profiling. Because racial or ethnic profiling should result in an overrepresentation of certain ethnic groups in police stops in a certain demographical area, an important first step would be to establish if that really is the case and, if so, what the exact numbers of this overrepresentation are per ethnic group. This is easier said than done because of the so-called "benchmark problem" (Ramirez, McDevitt & Farrell 2000; Walker 2001; Batton & Kadleck 2004; Engel & Calnon 2004). A fundamental difficulty is determining what benchmark to use in assessing whether the police target members of certain ethnic group disproportionately often. One has to compare the ethnic distribution of the people stopped in a particular area with a specific estimate of what would constitute proportionate stops. This estimate may be the resident population of an area, the people present in the area each day, people driving in or through the area etc. These numbers may differ significantly. To identify a good benchmark, one has to control for all of the variables affecting the distribution of the people targeted and it has reflect the same time and area from which data about police stops is to be collected. Obviously, the choice of the benchmark affects the conclusions to be drawn. Waddington, Stenson and Don (2004) state that, comparing with general population data in the US in generalis not an option because it ignores the fact that the police in their daily work on the street don't meet a representative sample of the population. Researchers also try to relate the number of stops to the "available population" at certain times and certain places (Lamberth 2006). Ideally one should be able to identify which people are and which people are not stopped, but this is not impossible in practice. That is why data on police stops is often linked with other data such as information on accidents, on observations of traffic mobility and are officers – and thus the outcomes of their stops – compared with each other and are outcomes of stops compared according to the various population groups (Ridgeway & McDonalds 2010). Even though over time these studies have provided useful insights, they have not solved the benchmark problem.

In addition to the benchmark problem, determining someone's ethno-racial background has proven to be a methodological ordeal. Whereas public and political debates often seem to unfold along the lines of "black and white," this doesn't do justice to the reality of a large – and ever-growing – group of people with a less clearly definable ethno-racial background. It is questionable whether law enforcement officials and researchers are always able to clearly distinguish and assess someone's ethno-racial background (Withrow 2010).

If there's one conclusion that can be drawn from the existing research, it is that the picture is not clear. Although a large part of the research points to racial disparity in police stops, a significant part of the research doesn't reveal this disparity at all. As Engel and Cohen (2014) rightfully observe in their overview mentioned above, most research does not explain the differences found. Decision-making processes or motivations behind certain actions aren't made transparent at all. Let it be clear that I am not trying to find ways to exculpate law enforcement officials from problematic police practices such as ethno-racial profiling. On the contrary, by critically reflecting upon the ways in which this practice has been measured so far, and by refining the methodologies that are predominantly used, I hope to contribute to a better understanding of the scope and the driving forces behind such a practice. A deeper understanding of these aspects is vital to paving the way for change. Tillyer and Engel (2012) argue that the time of non-theory-based quantitative research is over. They call for a stronger theoretical foundation to the question of why racial profiling would be taking place, and also state the necessity for more qualitative empirical studies focusing on decision-making processes in order to truly test for the possible theoretical explanations. I would like to underline this necessity. Proper qualitative research takes more time and uses more resources than quantitative research – time and resources being the two things that are mostly lacking when working in an academic setting – yet the value of rich qualitative data is priceless, especially when it comes to understanding complex processes with the many legal, organizational, personal, and circumstantial factors involved, including discretionary decision-making processes.

PRELIMINARY CONCLUSION II

This brings me to my second preliminary conclusion. The majority of police-citizen encounters occur in the absence of any outside supervision, and police officers therefore have a great deal of discretion throughout the decision-making processes leading up to and following an actual stop. Most of the social scientific research on police discretion focuses on the outcome of the decision to stop, search, or arrest a suspect, in other words, on Type A decisions taken at street level. However, studying and trying to make sense of these decisions, it is important to step back and examine what other decisions, motivations and perceptions precede the decision to stop someone, and within which social, legal, organizational, and personal context these decisions are made. Prior investigations on police discretion indicate that a combination of pre-existing attitudes, and the personality that a police officer develops through experiences on the job, only partly explain how officers respond in interactions with citizens (McBarnet 1981; Alpert & Dunham 2004; Stroshine, Alpert & Dunham 2008). In fact, empirical research indicates that police decision-making is primarily driven by situational factors related to criminal behavior (for example, the seriousness of the offense, victim requests and so on) and the administrative decision-making model – the legal and policy framework – under which the officer works (Worden 1989). Literature on the discretion of ordinary police officers did indeed establish early on that collective occupational norms, as well as law and formal policy, shape the way in which individual officers use their discretion (Skolnick 1966). In recent years, a wealth of research on decision-making processes has demonstrated how police decisions are complex processes involving a host of factors (Johnson & Morgan 2013). These include organizational and legal rules (Engel & Johnson 2006; Miller 2009), but also internal norms and values, including both conscious and subconscious stereotypes (Graham & Lowery 2004; Wilson et al. 2004). Evidently, police culture and occupational ideologies play an abiding role in informing officers about how they do their work, both through formal training and informal socialization processes (Loftus 2010).

Decisions related to criminal justice cannot to be fully understood unless they are considered in the broader socio-political background against which they are made; nor can they be understood unless all legal and organizational mandates that may influence street-level decisions are taken into consideration. Hawkins refers to the latter as the decision field in which these decisions are made (Hawkins 2003). In other words, Type A decisions are influenced by other Type A decisions as well as by a range of Type B – policy and legislative – decisions. Hawkins (2003) emphasizes how decisions regarding criminal justice are made in a rich and complex environment that acts as the setting for the shifting currents of broad political values and forces. He refers to this complex environment as the social surround, the broad and largely uncontrollable setting in which individual decision-making and the activities of the criminal justice bureaucracies in which such decision-making occurs take place. The social surround is influenced by much broader societal developments. The "decision field" is located in this social surround. Other than the social surround, the decision field is defined by and acted on by criminal justice bureaucracies. Whereas the law determines the contours and reach of the decision field, the decision field contains sets of policy and organizational ideas about how the ends of the law and formal policies are to be pursued. The decision field is therefore constructed by politicians and policymakers who create and shape these ideas and goals. This includes the official aims of laws and policy goals through to informal work instructions. The social surround and the decision field continuously interact, and together they influence the ways in which street-level officers will frame and decide on an individual case.

As is mostly the case in studies focusing on Type A discretionary decision-making, researchers have been concerned with the outcomes rather than figuring out the larger picture of what is producing and driving these outcomes. This research is correlational in character and is conducted using quantitative methods in which identified "factors" or "criteria" are statistically associated with decision outcomes. Although very valuable in identifying potentially relevant factors in decision-making processes, in shining insightful light on the practice of ethnic or racial profiling, this research has its limitations. Insofar as research aspires to influence or change criminal justice practices to any significant extent, analyses that fail to identify and unravel the complex nature of and context within which these practices take place, will not result in any changes at all. In doing so, these analyses might even contribute to the intensification of the very problematic practices they are trying to overturn.

4. BRINGING IT ALL TOGETHER AND LOOKING AHEAD

"The essence of ultimate decision remains impenetrable to the observer – often, indeed, to the decider himself (...) There will always be the dark and tangled stretches in the decision-making process – mysterious even to those who may be most intimately involved." – John Kennedy (as cited in Hammond, 1996)

I have argued that the concept of discretion not only offers interesting and also very natural – as opposed to artificial – opportunities for interdisciplinary research, but also that, in order to fully understand the dynamics and the impact of discretion and discretionary decision-making, it is in fact necessary to conduct interdisciplinary research. By drawing from my own research I aimed to show that both within more legally oriented and more empirically oriented research, analysis of criminal justice discretionary decision-making tends to take an individual case and the individual decision-maker – whether that's the legislature or the street-level police officer – as the primary unit of analysis when attempting to explain discretionary behavior. This individualistic view is incomplete, however, and fails to describe the real character of criminal justice decision-making, which has instead to be seen from a holistic or systemic perspective. In fact, while it may be obvious to see an individual as responsible for making a particular decision, a large part of discretionary decision-making related to criminal justice is a collective enterprise in which several national and international levels of people and/or institutions, be they formal or informal, may be part of the decision-making parties (Hawkins 1992,

2003). Nevertheless, while moving the research scope from the individual case towards a more systemic approach, we do need to remain aware – and therefore to constantly value and analyze – the role and influence of human agency acting within the criminal justice system as well. Besides the necessity for a more interdisciplinary and systemic approach to researching discretion and discretionary decision-making, I also advocate a more diverse demographical orientation in the current debates. As I have noted in the context of research on ethno-racial profiling, criminal justice and criminology debates tend to largely focus on the Global North, in particular on the United States and the United Kingdom, which raises the question of whether the research and its outcomes may reflect a form of Anglo-American exceptionalism. Without wanting to downplay the value and the importance of this research at all, on the contrary, it is necessary to be aware of the limitations of applying the outcomes to other national contexts and jurisdictions. This is especially the case when it comes to studying discretion and discretionary decision-making since the extent to which and the ways in which discretion is distributed, dealt with and perceived throughout the criminal justice system will differ significantly per jurisdiction. Although there may be similarities in the decision fields – international treaties, human rights, fundamental legal principles and so on – every country, or even every state when talking about the United States, will have unique criminal justice legislation and policies that will play a role in and affect the decision-making processes of those having to implement the legislation, enforce it or how citizens will perceive and fight against it. The same can be said for the social surround – the larger force field of social, economic and political forces.

In an attempt to get to the core of the crimmigration process – the merging of crime control and immigration control (Stumpf 2006; Eagly 2010; Cohn 2012; Chacón 2012; Hartry 2012; Siskin 2012; Sklansky 2012), a process which has somehow been driven by discretion, I intend to practice what I have preached here in my NWO-funded 5-year Vidi research project in the coming years.[6]

Although "crimmigration" was originally introduced as a term to describe certain developments that were taking place at the legislative and policy level – the creation of so-called crimmigration law (Stumpf 2006; Legomsky 2007; Miller 2004) – the meaning of the concept has expanded over the years to include the social and political context within which these legislative and policy changes take place (Van der Leun & Van der Woude 2014; Aas 2011) Part of studying the merging of crime control and migration control is includes analyzing how issues relating to crime and immigration are perceived and framed in the social and political context. Despite the clear complexity and multitude of forces driving the process of crimmigration, according to Motomura (2011) the discretion to stop persons is the strongest driver behind the process of crimmigration because it enables racial profiling and makes street-level officers

6 The NWO is the Netherlands Organisation for Scientific Research. The Innovational Research Incentives Scheme, Vidi, is a grant for experienced researchers. It allows researchers who have already spent several years doing postdoctoral research to develop their own innovative lines of research, and to appoint one or more researchers. My project is entitled "Getting to the Core of Crimmigration. Assessing the Role of Discretion in Managing Internal Cross-Border Mobility."

responsible for funneling immigrants into systems dealing with immigration crime or offenses. His assessment of the importance of street-level decision-making in the process of crimmigration is widely shared among scholars. Street-level discretionary decision-making in crimmigration studies is often complicated by the alleged link with racial profiling (Miller 2005; Stumpf 2006; Pratt 2008, 2010; Koulish 2010; Hernandez 2013). Although the process of racial profiling by law enforcement officials is unmistakably connected with the process of crimmigration, whether it can explain the process of crimmigration or whether it is an outcome of it, or both, remains unclear. Clarification depends on whether one approaches immigration control from a bottom-up or a top-down perspective (Lind 2015). In line with Motomura's assessment, the bottom-up method attributes a lot of power to the (Type A) decisions made at street level. Yet, in their assessment of the criminalization of migration, Provine and Doty (2011) observe that policy responses to unauthorized immigration reinforce racial anxieties by creating new discretionary spaces of enforcement within which these anxieties flourish and become institutionalized. In other words, although they do acknowledge the impact of racial anxiety at enforcement level, potentially leading to ethno-racial profiling, Provine and Doty see this is as the outcome of top-down (Type B) policy-level decisions. According to Sklansky (2012) the process of crimmigration cannot be seen as separate from the rising tendency of ad hoc instrumentalism that is visible within both criminal and administrative law. He defines ad hoc instrumentalism as "(...) a manner of thinking about law and legal institutions that downplays concerns about consistency and places little stock in formal legal categories, but instead sees legal rules and legal procedures simply as a set of interchangeable tools. In any given situation, faced with any given problem, officials are encouraged to use whichever tools are most effective against the person or persons causing the problem" (Sklansky 2012: 161). The underlying rationale behind the process of crimmigration seems to fit in with this tendency: in order to catch dangerous individuals – i.e. immigrants as well as criminals – a hybrid web of social control is spun in such a way that street-level law enforcement officials can choose between their criminal and administrative – immigration law – powers. Whichever route they take, crime control or migration control, it doesn't really matter as long as their actions are effective (Miller 2005; Stumpf 2006; Chacon 2012; Van der Woude; Van der Leun & Nijland 2014). Whereas Sklansky also attributes an important role to street-level decisions in driving the process of crimmigration, which is in line with Provine & Doty (2011), he explicitly places street-level actions against the background of broader changes in the control of crime and migration and, along with these, (Type B) decisions made in the upper legislative and policy echelons.

UNDERSTANDING EU INTERNAL BORDER POLICING THROUGH THE LENS OF DISCRETION

The core principles of the European Project, free movement, human rights, and solidarity are being put to the test in the wake of the refugee crisis and a range of terrorist attacks that have only further fuelled pre-existing anti-immigrant sentiments. In attempts to reclaim their national sovereignty, several European countries have resorted to far-reaching measures to control the right to enter and remain within national territories. Political leaders continue to assure the public that they can "secure the borders," eliminate unauthorized immigration and, by doing so, curb the risk of new terrorist attacks. Yet it is increasingly obvious that these are unachievable goals. Porous borders and transnational affiliations are realities of our times (Benhabib

2005). The call to put more "boots on the ground" in border areas has nevertheless become a potent political rallying cry in many nations of the world, reflecting widespread anxiety about national security and seemingly uncontrolled and uncontrollable changes in the economy and society. Although the current situation around immigration in Europe is extreme, as are some of the measures that have been taken to counter it, for over ten years members of the EU have increasingly relied on the tools, practices, logics, and rationales of the criminal justice system to respond to what the late Nils Christie called "suitable enemies." "Suitable enemies" stands for the anxieties brought on by globalization: mass mobility, economic restructuring, and other social dislocations (Christie 1986). Immigrants, foreign nationals, ethnic and racial minorities, and poor people have tended to bear the brunt of this transformation. Mobility itself has been subject to criminalization (Aliverti 2014) as immigration violations have become subject to criminal law and criminal penalties rather than to administration law (Stumpf 2006; Mitsilegas 2015). It is precisely this mixture of continuity with criminal justice history and the development of new forms and practices that students of border criminologies seek to understand and explain. Scholars have pointed out that the merging field of crimmigration control functions as a clear gatekeeper in terms of membership and access. On the one hand, this has resulted in borders "being everywhere" (Balibar 2002; Mutsaers 2014) and a wide range of non-traditional social control agents being drawn into the task of sorting out who belongs to a certain society and who does not (Guiraudon & Lahav 2000; Ambrosini & Van der Leun 2015). On the other hand, physical borders are once again being viewed as major tools of exclusion "(...) that can be strengthened and fostered to protect a community and a society against a phantasmic threat of otherness that tends to become flesh in the demonized and abject figure of a migrant or refugee" (Rajaram & Grundy-Warr 2007). At the border, a distinction is made between "bona fide" global citizens and "crimmigrant others" (Aas 2011, 2013; Barker 2012; Stumpf 2006; Van der Woude & Van Berlo 2015).

Figure 1: A holistic approach towards studying internal border policing

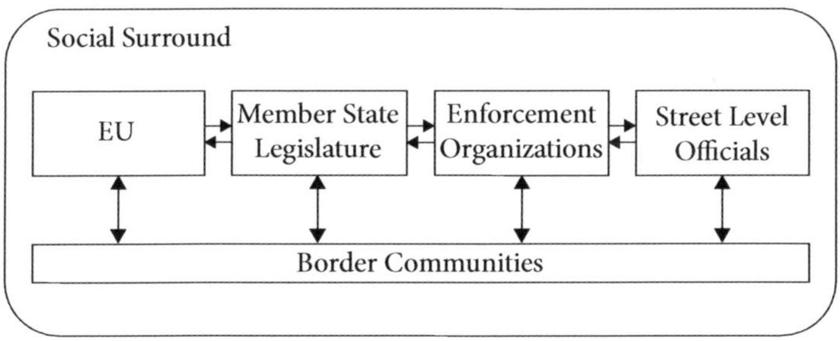

Over the next couple of years, I aim to shed light on the way in which different countries in Europe police potentially dangerous people moving across their internal borders. As illustrated by Figure 1, the project will adopt a multi-level and multi-actor approach towards discretion by focusing on the decisions made on the supranational, national, organizational and street level. Such a systemic assessment of discretionary decision-making may contribute to a better understanding of the process of crimmigration. This understanding – both in terms of why it is happening and in terms of how the process takes shape – is important to exploring ways in which the process and its often unjust outcomes could be overturned. Since the effects and success of discretionary decisions also rely heavily on the support for these decisions at a local level, in its assessment of the role discretion this project also includes the local – community – level and the way in which local communities perceive and act upon the discretionary decisions made by the actors at a national and supranational legislative, police and enforcement level. Are local communities able to react to and resist power at a national level? To what extent do these local communities use the discretion of border control officers and authorities to resist or perhaps even promote the process of crimmigration control?

These are important and challenging questions, questions that not only require an interdisciplinary and comparative approach, but questions that also require researchers to collaborate, which is something that does not always come naturally to them in the rather individualistic academic culture that is still dominated by the notion to "publish or perish." Working in the field of immigration, criminal justice and counterterrorism – matters that exceed national and disciplinary boundaries – I feel that the only way to make sense of what is going on the world today, and the only way things may change for the better, is by working together. I am therefore even more grateful to have received the Ada and Paul Cornil Prize, a prize that explicitly urges researchers in Leiden and Brussels to join forces.

5. SOME FINAL WORDS OF THANKS

By revealing my research agenda for the coming five years, I am nearing the end of my lecture, but not without some final words of thanks.

I would like once more to express my gratitude to Professor Sonja Snacken and Professor Kristel Beyens for nominating me, and also to thank the Crime and Society Research Group and the Vrije Universiteit Brussel for organizing a wonderful and festive award ceremony. These words of thanks also extent to Steven de Ridder, for being our long-time Belgian partner in crimmigration and a fitting representative of the Vrije Universiteit Brussels since he has been sowing the seeds for closer connections between both our universities and research groups over the past few years. I know that I speak on behalf of the Institute for Criminal Law & Criminology and the Van Vollenhoven Institute for Law, Governance and Development when I say that I – we – are looking forward to collaborating and working together on future research projects.

I would also like to thank several people who have been crucial to my academic career and for helping me to become the scholar that I am today.

First of all, my thanks go to Professor Martin Moerings and Professor Tineke Cleiren as my primary dissertation supervisors. Without both of you being willing to undertake this interdisciplinary journey with me while providing your ongoing support and advice, I wouldn't be where I am today. This truly feels like "our" achievement.

Secondly, my partner in crimmigration, without whom the duo "Van Der" would not exist: Professor Joanne van der Leun. Joanne, I cherish our bond and feel privileged working together with you. I am already looking forward to the many new adventurous projects and research trips that lie ahead of us.

I would also like to thank Professor Jan Crijns for taking on the risk of this highly competitive hybrid monster and allowing me the personal and academic space to develop further as a scholar, a teacher and an administrator.

While thanking those who have been important in my academic development, I would also like to acknowledge the importance of the Center for the Study of Law & Society (CSLS) at the University of California, Berkeley, and in particular Professor Jonathan Simon, Professor Malcolm Feeley and Professor Tony Platt for being a constant source of inspiration. It was during my time at the CSLS and during the many conversations I had, and still have, with you all that I learned to value the importance of socio-legal research and to truly embrace the fact that not fitting narrow pre-set disciplinary labels is actually something to be proud of. Lastly, I would like to thank the Leiden University Fund, the Schim van der Loeff Fund and the Gratama Foundation for so generously helping to fund my various research projects over the past couple of years.

REFERENCES

Aas, K.F. (2011) '"Crimmigrant" Bodies and Bona Fide Travelers: Surveillance, Citizenship and Global Governance'. *Theoretical Criminology* 15 (3), 331-346.

Aas, K.F. (2013) 'The Ordered and the Bordered Society: Migration Control, Citizenship, and the Northern Penal State'. In: K.F. Aas & M. Bosworth (eds.) *The Borders of Punishment: Migration, Citizenship and Social Exclusion*, Oxford, UK: Oxford University Press: 21-39.

Aas, K.F. (2014) 'Bordered Penality: Precarious Membership and Abnormal Justice'. *Punishment & Society* 16 (5), 520-541.

Agamben, G. (1998) *Homo Sacer: Sovereign Power and Bare Life*, translated by Daniel Heller-Roazen. Stanford: Stanford University Press.

Agamben, G. (2001) 'On Security and Terror', *Frankfurter Allgemeine Zeitung*, 20 September 2001.

Agamben, G. (2003) *Etat d'Exception: Homo Sacer II, 1*, Paris: Seuil.

Agamben, G. (2004) *State of Exception*, translated by Kevin Attell. Chicago: Chicago University Press.

Aliverti, A.J. (2013) *Crimes of Mobility: Criminal Law and the Regulation of Immigration*. London: Routledge.

Alpert, G. & Duham, R. (2004) *Understanding Police Use of Force. Officers, Suspects, and Reciprocity*. Cambridge: Cambridge University Press.

Altheide, D.L. (2003) 'Notes towards a Politics of Fear'. *Journal of Crime, Conflict and Media* (1) 37-54.

Ambrosini, M. & Van der Leun, J.P. (2015) 'Introduction to the Special Issue: Implementing Human Rights: Civil Society and

Migration Policies'. *Journal of Immigrant and Refugee Studies* 13 (2), 103-115.

Baldwin, R. & Hawkins, K. (1984) 'Discretionary Justice: Davis Reconsidered'. *Public Law (winter)*, 570-599.

Balibar, E. (2002) *Politics and the Other Scene*. London: Verso.

Barker, V. (2012) 'Global Mobility and Penal Order: Criminalizing Migration, A View from Europe'. *Sociology Compass* 6 (2), 113-121.

Barnes, B. (1995) *The Elements of Social Theory*. London: UCL Press.

Bauman, Z. (2000) *Liquid Modernity*. Cambridge: Polity Press.

Beck, U. (1992) *The Risk Society. Towards a New Modernity*. London: Sage.

Beck, U. (2002) 'The Terrorist Threat. World Risk Society Revisited'. *Theory, Culture & Society, 19* (4), 39-41.

Bell, J. (1992) 'Discretionary Decision-Making. A Jurisprudential View'. In: K. Hawkins (ed.), *The Uses of Discretion*. Oxford: Clarendon Press, 89-111.

Benhabib, S. (2005) *The Rights of Others: Aliens, Residents and Citizens*. Cambridge, UK: Cambridge University Press.

Black, J. (1997) *Rules and Regulators*. Oxford: Oxford University Press.

Black, J. (2001) 'Managing Discretion'. *ARLC Conference Papers Penalties: Policy, Principles and Practice in Government Regulation*. Accessible via: www.lse.ac.uk/collections/law/staff%20publications%20full%20text/black/alrc%20managing%20discretion.pdf.

Bootsma, P. (2000) *De Molukse Acties; Treinkapingen en Gijzelingen, 1970-1978*, Amsterdam: Boom.

Bovenkerk, F. (2014) '"Twee Marokkanen op een scooter? Die houd ik aan." Ethnic profiling in Nederland. In: M. Davidovic & A.B. Terlouw (red.), *Diversiteit & Discriminatie. Onderzoek naar processen van in- en uitsluiting.* Amsterdam: Amsterdam University Press, 203-222.

Brownlee, I. (1998) 'New Labour – New Penology? Punitive Rhetoric and the Limits of managerialism in Criminal Justice Policy'. *Journal of Law and Society* 25 (3), 313-335.

Bushway, S.D. & Forst, B. (2013) 'Studying Discretion in the Processes that Generate Criminal Justice Sanctions'. *Justice Quarterly*, 30:2, 199-222.

Çankaya, S. (2012a) *De controle van marsmannetjes en ander schorriemorrie: Het beslissingsproces tijdens proactief politiewerk*. Den Haag: Boom Lemma.

Chacón, J.M. (2009) 'Managing Migration Through Crime'. *Columbia Law Review* 109: 135-184. UC Irvine School of Law Research Paper No. 2015-12. Available at SSRN: http://ssrn.com/abstract=2553535.

Chacón, J.M. (2012) 'Overcriminalizing Immigration'. *Journal of Criminal Law & Criminology* 102 (3), 613-652.

Cheliotis, L.K. (2006) 'How Iron Is the Iron Cage of New Penology? The Role of Human Agency in the Implementation of Criminal Justice Policy'. *Punishment & Society*, 8 (3), 313-340.

Christie, N. (1986) 'Suitable Enemy'. In: H. Bianchi & R. van Swaaningen (eds.), *Abolitionism: Toward a Non-Repressive Approach to Crime*. Amsterdam: Free University Press.

Coenders, M. et al. (2009) 'Discriminatie-ervaringen. Een onderzoek naar ervaren discriminatie op grond van land van herkomst, geloof en huidskleur'. In: I. Boog, W. Dinsbach, J. van Donselaar & P.R. Rodrigues (red.) *Monitor Rassendiscriminatie 2009*. Den Haag: Art. 1, p. 33-74.

Cohen, S. (1979) 'The Punitive City: Notes on the Dispersal of Social Control'. *Contemporary Crises* 3 (4), 339-363.

Cohen, S. (1985) *Visions of Social Control*, Cambridge: Polity Press.

Davis, K.C. (1969) *Discretionary Justice: A Preliminary Inquiry.* University of Utah.

Davis, K.C. (1975) *Discretionary Justice in Europe and America*, Urbana: University of Illinois Press.

De Giorgi, A. (2014, August 21) 'Ferguson and beyond: "Justifiable Homicides" and Premature Death in the Urban Ghetto'. *Social Justice blog*, from www.socialjusticejournal.org/?p=2455.

Dekkers, T. & Woude, M.A.H., van der (2014) '"Staring at the Felony Forest". De complexiteit van risicoprofilering nader in kaart gebracht'. *Proces* 93 (1), 52-70.

Dworkin, R.M. (1977) *Taking Rights Seriously.* Cambridge Massachusetts: Harvard University Press.

Eagly, I. (2011) 'Local Immigration Prosecution: A Study of Arizona before SB 1070'. *UCLA Law Review* 58: 1749-1817.

Emerson, R.M. (1983) 'Holistic Effects in Social Control Decision-Making'. *Law & Society Review* 17: 425-455.

Emerson, R.M. & Paley, B. (1992) 'Organizational Horizons and Complaint Filing'. In: K. Hawkins (ed.), *The Uses of Discretion*, Oxford: Clarendon Press.

EU FRA (2009) European Union Minorities and Discrimination Survey (EU-MIDIS) (2009) Main results report.

Feeley, M.F. & Simon, J. (1992) 'The New Penology: Notes on the Emerging Strategy of Corrections and Its Implications'. *Criminology* 30 (4), 449-474.

Galligan, D.J. (1986, 1990) *Discretionary Powers. A Legal Study of Official Discretion*, Oxford: Clarendon Press.

Garland, D. (2000) '"The Culture of High Crime Societies: Some preconditions of recent "law and order" policies'. *British Journal of Criminology* 40 (3), 347-375.

Garland, D. (2001) *The Culture of Control: Crime and Social Order in Contemporary Society.* Oxford: Oxford University Press.

Garland, D. & Sparks, R. (2000) 'Criminology, Social Theory and the Challenge of Our Times'. *British Journal of Criminology*, 40: 189-204, p. 201.
Gelsthorpe, L. & Padfield, N. (eds.) (2003) *Exercising Discretion. Decision-Making in the Criminal Justice System and beyond.* London: Routledge.
Gelsthorpe, L. & Padfield, N. (2003) 'Introduction'. In: L. Gelsthorpe & N. Padfield (eds.), *Exercising Discretion. Decision-Making in the Criminal Justice System and beyond.* London: Routledge, 1-28.
Giddens, A. (1999) 'Risk and Responsibility'. *Modern Law Review* 62 (1), 1-10.
Goffman, E. (1959) *The Presentation of Self in Everyday Life*, New York: Anchor Books.
Guiraudon, V. & Lahav, G. (2000) 'A Reappraisal of the State Sovereignty Debate The Case of Migration Control'. *Comparative Political Studies* 33 (2), 163-195.
Handler, J.F. (1986) *The Conditions of Discretion: Autonomy, Community, Bureaucracy.* New York: Russel Sage Foundation.
Hawkins, K. (1986) 'On Legal Decision-Making'. *Washington and Lee Law Review* 42 (4), 1161-1242.
Hawkins, K. (1992) 'The Use of Legal Discretion: Perspectives from Law & Social Science'. In: K. Hawkins (ed.), *The Uses of Discretion.* Oxford: Clarendon Press.
Hawkins, K. (2002) *Law as Last Resort: Prosecution Decision-Making in a Regulatory Agency.* Oxford: Oxford University Press.
Hawkins, K. (2003) 'Order, Rationality and Silence: Some Reflections on Criminal Justice Decision-Making'. In: L. Gelsthorpe & N. Padfield (eds.), *Exercising Discretion. Decision-Making in the Criminal Justice System and beyond.* London: Routledge, 186-219.

Hernandez, C.C.G. (2013) 'Creating Crimmigration'. *Brigham Young University Law Review* 6, 1457-1516.

Hough, M. (2013) 'Procedural justice and professional policing in times of austerity'. *Criminology and Criminal Justice*, 13 (2), 181-197.

Hough, M., Jackson, J., Bradford, B., Myhill, A. & Quinton, P. (2010) 'Procedural Justice, Trust, and Institutional Legitimacy'. *Policing: A Journal of Policy and Practice* 4 (3), 203-210. doi: 10.1093/police/paq027.

Hudson, B. (2003) *Justice in the Risk Society*, London: Sage Publications.

Hupe, P. (2013) 'Dimensions of Discretion: Specifying the Object of Street-Level Bureaucracy Research'. *dms – der moderne Staat – Zeitschrift fur Public Policy, Recht und Management* 6 (2), 425-440.

Janse, R. (2005) 'Fighting Terrorism in the Netherlands; a Historical Perspective'. *Utrecht Law Review* 1 (1), 55-67.

Jewell, C.J. & Glaser, B.E. (2006) 'Toward a General Analytical Framework: Organizational Setting, Policy Goals and Street-Level Behavior'. *Administration and Society* 38 (3), 335-364.

Johnson, R.R. & Morgan, M.A. (2013) 'Suspicion Formation among Police Officers: An International Literature Review'. *Criminal Justice Studies: A Critical Journal of Crime, Law and Society* 26 (1), 99-114.

Kanstroom, D. (1997) 'Surrounding the Hole in the Doughnut: Discretion and Deference in U.S. Immigration Law'. *Tulane Law Review* 71, 703-818.

Kemshall, H. (2003) *Understanding Risk in Criminal Justice*. Berkshire: Open University Press.

Kennedy, R. (1997) *Race, Crime, and the Law*. New York, NY: Pantheon.

Kleijer-Kool, L. (2013) *Multicultureel politiewerk*. Den Haag: Boom Lemma uitgevers.

Lynch, M. (1998) 'Waste Managers? The New Penology, Crime Fighting, and Parole Agent Identity'. *Law and Society Review* 32 (4), 839-869.

Leun, J.P., van der, & Woude, M.A.H. van der, Vijverberg R.D., Vrijhoef R.P.M. & Leupen, A.J. (2014) *Etnisch profileren in Den Haag? Een verkennend onderzoek naar beslissingen en opvattingen op straat*. Den Haag: Boom Lemma uitgevers.

Maynard-Moody, S. & Musheno, M. (2003) *Cops, Teachers, Counselors: Stories from the Front Lines of Public Service*. Ann Arbor: The University of Michigan Press.

Maynard-Moody, S. & Portillo, S. (2010) 'Street-Level Bureaucracy Theory'. In: R.F. Durant & G.C. Edwards III (eds.), *The Oxford Handbook of American Bureaucracy*, Oxford: Oxford University Press, 252-277.

Mazerolle, L. et al. (2014) *Procedural Justice and Legitimacy in Policing*, London: Springer International Publishing.

Meyers, M.K. & Lehmann Nielsen, V. (2012) 'Street-Level Bureaucrats and the Implementation of Public Policy'. In: B. Guy Peters & J. Pierre (eds), *The SAGE Handbook of Public Administration*, London: SAGE, 305-318 (second edition).

McCulloch, J. & Pickering, S. (2009) 'Pre-Crime and Counter-terrorism. Imagining Future Crime in "the War on Terror"'. *British Journal of Criminology* 49, 628-645.

Mensah, K.B. (1998) 'Legal Control of Discretionary Powers in Ghana: Lessons from English Administrative Law Theory'. *Afrika Focus* 14 (2), 119-140.

Miller, T.A. (2005) 'Blurring the Boundaries between Immigration and Crime Control after September 11th'. *Boston College Third World Law Journal* 25 (1), 81-123.

Mitsilegas, V. (2015) *The Criminalisation of Migration in Europe: Challenges for Human Rights and the Rule of Law.* London: Springer.
Motomura, H. (2011) 'Federal Immigration Enforcement and State and Local Arrests'. *UCLA Law Review* 58, 1819-1858.
Motomura, H. (2014) *The President's Discretion, Immigration Enforcement & the Rule of Law.* American Immigration Council.
Munster, R. van (2004) 'The War on Terrorism: When the Exception Becomes the Rule'. *International Journal for the Semiotics of Law* 17.
Musheno, M. (1986) 'The Justice Motive in the Social Policy Process: Searching for Normative Rules of Distribution'. *Policy Studies Review* 5, 697-704.
Mutsaers, P. (2014) 'An Ethnographic Study of the Policing of Internal Borders in the Netherlands. Synergies between Criminology and Anthropology'. *British Journal of Criminology* 54 (5), 831-848.
Mutsaers, P. (2015) *A Public Anthropology of Policing. Law Enforcement and Migrants in the Netherlands.* Dissertation, Tilburg University.
Padfield, N., Liebling, A. & Arnold, H. (2003) 'Discretion and the Release of Life Sentence Prisoners'. In: L. Gelsthorpe & N. Padfield (eds.), *Exercising Discretion. Decision-Making in the Criminal Justice System and beyond.* London: Routledge, 186-219.
Pratt, A. (2010) 'Between a Hunch and a Hard Place: Making Suspicion Reasonable at the Canadian Border'. *Social & Legal Studies* 19, 461-480.
Pratt, A. & Thompson, S.K. (2008) 'Chivalry, Race and Discretion at the Canadian Border'. *British Journal of Criminology* 48, 620-640.

Prosser, T. (1982) 'Towards a Critical Public Law'. *British Journal of Law & Society* 9, 1-4.
Prottas, J.D. (1979) *People Processing: The Street-Level Bureaucrat in Public Service Bureaucracies*. Lexington, Mass: D.C. Heath.
Rajaram, P.K. & Grundy-Warr, C. (2007) 'Introduction'. In: P.K. Rajaram & C. Grundy-Warr (eds.), *Borderscapes*. Minneapolis, MN: University of Minnesota Press.
Reitz, K. (1998) 'Modeling Discretion in American Sentencing Systems'. *Law and Policy* 20 (4), 389-428.
Robert, D. (2001) 'Transformations récentes de la législation fédérale sur la mise en liberté sous condition au Canada. Une lecture à la lumière des écrits sur la notion de risque'. *Criminologie* 34 (1), 73-99.
Schneider, C.E. (1992) 'Discretion and Rules: A Lawyer's View'. In: K. Hawkins (ed.), *The Uses of Discretion*. Oxford: Clarendon Press.
Schneider, C.L. (2008) 'Police Power and Race Riots in Paris'. *Politics and Society* 36 (1), 133-159.
Simon, J. (2007) *Governing Through Crime. How the War on Crime Transformed American Democracy and Created a Culture of Fear*. Oxford: Oxford University Press.
Simon, J. (2014, August 25) 'Ferguson and Human Dignity'. *Social Justice blog*, from www.socialjusticejournal.org/?p=2491.
Simon, J. & Feeley, M.F. (1994) 'Actuarial Justice: The Emerging New Criminal Law'. In: D. Nelken (ed.), *The Futures of Criminology*, London: Sage.
Simon, J. & Feeley, M. (2003) 'The Form and Limits of the New Penology'. In: T. Blomberg & S. Cohen (eds.), *Punishment and Social Control*, Aldine De Gruyter, New York, 75-116.
Sklansky, D.A. (2012) 'Crime, Immigration and Ad Hoc Instrumentalism'. *New Criminal Law Review* 15, 157-223.

Slingeneyer, T. (2010) 'The New Penology: A Grid for Analyzing the Transformations of Penal Discourses, Techniques and Objectives'. *Champ pénal/Penal field* [En ligne], Vol. IV | 2007 (mis en ligne le 27 février 2010, consulté le 19 juillet 2016).

Solomos, J. (2011) 'Race, Rumours and Riots: Past, Present and Future'. *Sociological Research Online* 16 (4). www.socresonline.org.uk/16/4/20.html.

Spader, D.J. (1984) 'Rule of Law V. Rule of Man: The Search for the Golden Zigzag between Conflicting Fundamental Values'. *Journal of Criminal Justice* 12, 379-394.

Stroshine, M., Alpert, G. & Dunham, R. (2008) 'The Influence of "Working Rules" on Police Suspicion and Discretionary Decision-Making'. *Police Quarterly* 11, 315-337.

Stumpf, J. (2006) 'The Crimmigration Crisis: Immigrants, Crime and Sovereign Power'. Bepress Legal Series: Working Paper 1635, Berkley, Bepress Legal Repository, http://law.bepress.com/expresso/eps/1635.

Stumpf, J. (2015) 'D(e)volving Discretion: Lessons from the Life and Times of Secure Communities'. *American University Law Review* 64, 1259-1284.

Svensson, J., Sollie, H., & Saharso, S. (2012) *Proactief handhaven en gelijk behandelen*. Amsterdam: Reed Business.

Svensson, J. & Saharso, S. (2014) 'Proactive Policing and Equal Treatment of Ethnic-Minority Youths'. *Policing & Society: An International Journal of Research and Policy* 25 (4), 393-408.

Stumpf, J.P. (2006) 'The Crimmigration Crisis: Immigrants, Crime, & Sovereign Power'. Bepress Legal Series, 1635.

Stumpf, J.P. (2011) 'Doing Time: Crimmigration Law and the Perils of Haste'. *UCLA Law Review* 58, 1705.

Stuntz, W.J. (2011) *The Collapse of American Criminal Justice*, Cambridge: The Belknap Press of Harvard University Press.

Sunshine, J. & Tyler, T.R. (2003) 'The Role of Procedural Justice and Legitimacy in Shaping Public Support for Policing', *Law & Society Review* 37 (5), 13-48.

Suyver Committee (Commissie Evaluatie Antiterrorisme-maatregelen) (2009) *Naar een integrale evaluatie van Anti-terrorismemaatregelen*, Den Haag: SDU Uitgevers.

Tankebe, J. & Liebling, A. (eds.) (2013) *Legitimacy and Criminal Justice. An International Exploration.* Oxford: Oxford University Press.

Tyler, T.R. (2003) 'Procedural Justice, Legitimacy and the Effective Rule of Law'. *Crime and Justice* 30, 283-357.

Tyler, T.R. & Blader, S.L. (2003) 'The Group Engagement Model: Procedural Justice, Social Identity and Cooperative Behavior'. *Personality and Social Psychology Review* 7 (4), 349-361.

Tyler, T.R. & Wakslak, C.J. (2004) 'Profiling and Police Legitimacy: Procedural Justice, Attributions of Motive, and Acceptance of Police Authority'. *Criminology* 42 (2), 253-282.

Unger, R.M. (1976) *Law in Modern Society*, Free Press.

Veer, L. van der, Sluis, A. van, Van de Walle, S. & Ringeling, A. (2013) *Vertrouwen in de politie: trends en verklaringen, Een studie voor het Programma Politie en Wetenschap.*

Woude, M.A.H. van der (2010), *Wetgeving in een Veiligheidscultuur. Totstandkoming van antiterrorismewetgeving bezien van maatschappelijke en (rechts)politieke context.* Den Haag: Boom Juridische uitgevers.

Woude, M.A.H. van der (2012) 'Tegen Dovenmansoren? Een verkennend onderzoek naar percepties over de onderlinge communicatie tussen strafrechtswetenschap en wetgever met het oog op de kwaliteit van strafwetgeving'. In: *De spanningsrelatie tussen feiten, wetenschap en wetgeving.* Nijmegen: Wolf Legal Publishers, 1-72.

Woude, M.A.H. van der (2012a) 'Dutch Counterterrorism: An Exceptional Body of Legislation or Just an Inevitable Product of the Culture of Control?' In: G. Molier & A. Ellian (eds.), *The State of Exception in a Time of Terror*. Dordrecht: Republic of Letters Publishing, 69-95.

Woude, M.A.H. van der (2012b) 'De erfenis van 10 jaar strafrechtelijke terrorismebestrijding in Nederland'. *Strafblad* 9-18.

Woude, M.A.H. van der & Berlo, P. van (2015) 'Crimmigration at the Internal Borders of Europe? Examining the Schengen Governance Package'. *Utrecht Law Review* 11 (1), 61-79.

Woude, M.A.H. van der, Brouwer, J. & Dekkers T.J.M. (2016) *Beslissen in grensgebieden. Een onderzoek naar het Mobiel Toezicht Veiligheid zoals uitgevoerd door de Koninklijke Marechaussee*. Den Haag: Boom criminologie.

Woude, M.A.H. van der, Leun, J.P. van der & Nijland, J.A. (2014) 'Crimmigration in the Netherlands'. *Law and Social Inquiry* 39 (3), 560-579.

ABOUT THE ADA & PAUL CORNIL PRIZE

The Ada and Paul Cornil Prize is the result of a bequest from Mrs. Ada Cornil, which is given to the Vrije Universiteit Brussel (Free University Brussels) in memory of her husband Paul Cornil to support the study of criminal policy and criminological sociology. Paul Cornil (1903 - 1985) had a doctorate in literature and philosophy and a doctorate in law and was married to Ada Sand. In 1946, Paul Cornil was appointed Secretary General of the Ministry of Justice of Belgium, a position he would hold until 1968. In this capacity, Paul Cornil laid the foundation for a number of important reforms to the Belgian criminal justice system. Parallel to this he also built an academic career for himself, teaching courses in criminology, penology and criminal law. He finished his academic career as chairman of the School of Criminology at the VUB, known today as the Department of Criminology. After his death, Mrs Ada Cornil wanted the legacy of her husband to go on living through the bequest she gave to the university; as a result the Ada and Paul Cornil Prize was created. According to the rules of the prize the VUB"s Department of Criminology must award this prize to "a renowned foreign researcher with outstanding scientific merits in the field of criminological sociology or criminal policy, who also wants to build a joint research project with researchers in criminology at the Vrije Universiteit Brussel."

ABOUT THE AUTHOR

Maartje van der Woude is a graduate of Leiden University the Netherlands, where she obtained her LL.B and LL.M in Criminal Law (both with distinction) as well as her B.Sc and M.Sc. Criminology (both cum laude). In December 2010 she successfully defended her dissertation "Legislation in a Culture of Control. The Drafting of Dutch Counterterrorism Legislation Seen from a Social and Legal-Political Context" (Boom Juridische uitgevers, The Hague). Part of her dissertation research was carried out at the Center for the Study of Law and Society (University of California, in Berkeley), where Van der Woude was a visiting research scholar in the spring of 2008.

Professor Van der Woude's expertise lies with legal and social matters related to terrorism and counterterrorism, border security and immigration, and the growing interconnectedness of all four. This process is also referred to as crimmigration or the securitization of migration. Her current research on border control and border communities in the EU, for which Professor Van der Woude was granted one of the competitive Vidi grants issued by the Netherlands Organisation for Scientific Research (NWO), takes an interdisciplinary approach by focusing both on the legal normative questions as well as the empirical questions. By studying the political discourse and legislation at the level of the EU as well as at Member State level, Van der Woude aims to provide insight into the interaction and complex dynamics between the level of supranational decision-making and the level of national decision-making. Who are the actors responsible for border control decisions, and what are the political and humanitarian interests at stake? To what extent do the decisions at a supranational level leave discretionary space for Member States in the further development of specific rules and regulations? And, while delving deeper, how do these rules and regulations on internal border control play out at street level? Together with two PhD students, she recently finished a case study of the Netherlands for which the team spent over 800 hours in the field with the Royal Netherlands Military Constabulary (Koninklijke Marechaussee), which is the authority responsible for border control. Boom criminologie have published the results of this study in Dutch (*Beslissen in Grensgebieden*, 2016).

Professor Van der Woude is currently affiliated as professor of Sociology of Law with the Van Vollenhoven Institute for Law, Governance and Society and as an associate professor of Criminal Law with the Institute for Criminal Law & Criminology, both at Leiden Law School, the Netherlands. She teaches courses in Criminal Law, Criminology, Criminal Justice and Sociology of Law. In her capacity as a visiting professor, Van der Woude also taught at Hastings College of the Law (San Francisco, California) in the spring of 2014, and at the University of Maryland (College Park, Maryland) in the spring of 2016. In her urge to bring together the "law in the books" with "the law in action", Professor van der Woude is continuously seeking to combine her work in academia with the actual practice of law and law enforcement. She does so not only by carefully choosing and participating in her empirical research, but also by working as a deputy judge at the District Court of Noord-Holland.